G. SCHIRMER OPERA ANTHOLOGY

ARIAS FOR
MEZZO-SOPRANO

Compiled and Edited by
Robert L. Larsen

ISBN 978-0-7935-0401-5

G. SCHIRMER, Inc.

DISTRIBUTED BY

HAL•LEONARD®
CORPORATION
7777 W. BLUEMOUND RD. P.O. BOX 13819 MILWAUKEE, WI 53213

ROBERT L. LARSEN, editor and compiler of this anthology series, brings to the project experience from both professional opera and the academic realm. He is founder and artistic director of one of America's major opera festivals, the critically acclaimed Des Moines Metro Opera, and since the company's founding in 1973 has been conductor and stage director for all of its main stage productions. Since 1965 he has also been chairman of the department of music at Simpson College in Indianola, Iowa, and during his tenure the department has received national recognition and awards for its serious and extensive program of operatic training for undergraduates. Dr. Larsen holds a bachelor's degree from Simpson College, a master's degree in piano performance from the University of Michigan, and a doctoral degree in opera conducting from Indiana University. He is highly regarded as an opera coach and accompanist, and has assisted in the training of many artists with significant operatic careers.

The editor wishes to dedicate these volumes to the memory of Douglas Duncan, colleague and friend.

Editorial Advisor: Richard Walters
Aria Text Editor and Translator: Martha Gerhart
Assistant Editors: Patrick Hansen, William Casey
Music Engraving: Sangji International

On the cover: "L'opéra de Paris" by Raoul Dufy
Used by permission of The Phillips Collection, Washington, D.C.

CONTENTS

FOREWORD

It has been a pleasure to reflect on the enormous repertory that the world of opera affords, and to choose from it a group of important and representative arias for soprano, mezzo-soprano, tenor, baritone, and bass to be included in these anthologies of opera arias.

In making these selections, I confess that I have not applied a constant criterion or standard, but rather have chosen to alter my perspective with each volume. All of these collections are intended to be of particular use to students and teachers of voice. Thus the soprano volume, for example, concentrates on lyric arias, rather than venturing very far into the rich material for coloratura, spinto, or dramatic voices.

The other volumes include the lyric arias most often sung by student voices, but also include other significant arias for a voice-type. For instance, I can't imagine a young baritone who would not be inspired by looking through the wonder of the Prologue from *I Pagliacci* within the confines of his practice room, or a tenor who doesn't anticipate with excitement the day when "Che gelida manina" may fit his voice like a glove. On the other hand, I have omitted some important repertory, such as many of the great Verdi baritone arias, because they are widely available, and are certainly the province of only the most experienced performer. Instead, I have chosen pieces of value not previously found in such collections, including arias in English for each voice-type.

Each aria has been painstakingly researched in preparing these new editions, creating what I believe will be an eminently credible and useful source for this music. There are countless incidents where notes or words have been corrected to create a more substantiated presentation than in previous editions. Throughout the collections, one will find many spots where traditional cadenzas are recommended. Appropriate appoggiaturas, as defined by conservative application of tradition, are indicated as well. There are instances where an entirely revised piano reduction, more representative of the full score, has been created.

These anthologies are for all of us who must remain students of our art throughout our lifetimes. I'm a vocal coach and opera conductor who believes firmly in exposing the gifted performer to the firmament, being sure that he or she understands that each star must be attained at its own special time, to be plucked and polished again and again throughout a musical career. Among these arias may be the first one ever studied, but if it's by someone destined to be a real singer, it will remain in mind and heart forever.

Robert L. Larsen
March, 1991

NOTES and TRANSLATIONS

Translator's Note

My aim in providing these "literal" translations was to give accurate line-by-line translations, as opposed to word-by-word translations. At the same time, the goal was to translate a true sense of the thought of each word or phrase.

In this format, therefore, the words on each line of original language text correspond to the words on each line of translation. Whenever, for contextual and idiomatic reasons, a line-by-line format into English is not possible, the printing is indented. In such cases, the whole idea of the indented foreign-language text segment corresponds to the whole idea of the indented English translation segment.

There are many antiquated and poetic word forms in opera texts which appear in various usages. In editing the aria texts various punctuation was discovered in various sources. When challenged by discrepancies, I have made justifiable choices for this edition. In some cases the punctuation has been modernized in the interest of clarity or consistency.

M. G.

NOTES and TRANSLATIONS

The arias are presented chronologically by year of first performance.

DIDO AND AENEAS

1689
music by Henry Purcell
libretto by Nahum Tate (after Virgil's *Aeneid*, iv)

When I am laid in earth

from Act III
setting: Carthage, after the Trojan War; outside the palace dwelling of Dido, queen of Carthage
character: Dido

Dido and Aeneas, written for a girls' school in Chelsea, is the first real opera in the English language. In the opera's concluding moments Dido sings this great air, which is composed over a ground bass. She has discovered that the Trojan Aeneas has deserted her to pursue his destiny as the founder of Rome. With her attendants about her, she prepares to mount her funeral pyre.

ORFEO ED EURIDICE

1762
music by Christoph Willibald von Gluck
libretto by Raniero de' Calzabigi (based on Greek mythology)

Che farò senza Euridice?

from Act III, scene 1
setting: Mythology; a region between the Elysian fields and the earth
character: Orfeo

Orfeo, whose wife Euridice died and was taken to the Underworld, pursues her to the gates of Hades where his songs enchant the Furies. He wins her release on the condition that he will not look at her until they have escaped the nether regions. But, when she pleads for a single glance and refuses to follow him further, he defies the gods and takes her in his arms. She dies, and he sings this beautiful lament.

Ahimè! Dove trascorsi?	*Alas! Where have I traversed?*
Dove mi spinse un delirio d'amor?	*Where has a delirium of love thrust me?*
Sposa! Euridice! Consorte!	*Bride! Euridice! Wife!*
Ah, più non vive! La chiamo in van.	*Ah, she lives no more; I call her in vain.*
Misero me, la perdo	*Wretched me—I lose her*
e di nuovo e per sempre!	*once again and forever!*
Oh legge! Oh morte!	*Oh law! Oh death!*
Oh ricordo crudel!	*Oh cruel memory!*
Non ho soccorso,	*I do not have help;*
non m'avanza consiglio!	*counsel does not come forth for me!*
Io veggo solo	*I see only*
(oh fiera vista!)	*(oh savage sight!)*
il luttuoso aspetto	*the sad aspect*
dell'orrido mio stato.	*of my horrible state.*
Saziati, sorte rea:	*Be satisfied, wicked fate:*
son disperato!	*I am without hope!*

The historical notes and synopses in this section are by the editor; translations are by Martha Gerhart.

Che farò senza Euridice?
Dove andrò senza il mio ben?
Che farò? Dove andrò?
Che farò senza il mio ben?
Euridice! Oh Dio! Rispondi!
Io son pure il tuo fedel.
Ah! non m'avanza più soccorso,
   più speranza
     nè dal mondo, nè dal ciel!

What will I do without Euridice?
Where will I go without my beloved?
What will I do? Where will I go?
What will I do without my beloved?
Euridice! Oh God! Answer!
I am still your faithful one.
Ah, no more help, no more hope
   for me comes forth
     from earth, nor from heaven!

LE NOZZE DI FIGARO

(The Marriage of Figaro)
1786
music by Wolfgang Amadeus Mozart
libretto by Lorenzo da Ponte (after *La Folle Journée, ou Le Mariage de Figaro*, a comedy by Pierre Augustin Caron de Beaumarchais)

Non so più cosa son

from Act I
setting: near Seville, the 17th century; the palace of Count Almaviva: Figaro and Susanna's new room, not yet completely furnished
character: Cherubino

Cherubino, the teenage page to Count Almaviva, enters and complains to Susanna, the Countess' chamber maid, that the Count has just caught him embracing Barbarina and plans to banish him from the castle. All thought of his plight is forgotten, however, when he sees a ribbon belonging to the Countess, with whom he is smitten. He snatches it, giving Susanna in exchange the manuscript of one of his songs. He tells her to sing it everywhere, proclaiming his passion for all women and his love affair with love.

Non so più cosa son, cosa faccio;
or di foco, ora sono di ghiaccio.
Ogni donna cangiar di colore,
   ogni donna mi fa palpitar.
Solo ai nomi d'amor, di diletto,
mi si turba, mi s'altera il petto,
e a parlare mi sforza d'amore un desio,
   un desio ch'io non posso spiegar.
Parlo d'amor vegliando,
parlo d'amor sognando,
all'acqua, all'ombra, ai monti,
ai fiori, all'erbe, ai fonti,
all'eco, all'aria, ai venti,
che il suon de' vani accenti
   portano via con se.
E se non ho chi m'oda,
parlo d'amor con me.

I don't know anymore what I am, what I'm doing;
now I'm made of fire, now of ice.
Every woman makes me change color;
   every woman makes me tremble.
At merely the words "love," "pleasure,"
my breast becomes nervous and upset,
and a desire for love—a desire that I
   can't explain—forces me to talk.
I talk about love when awake;
I talk about love when dreaming—
to the water, to the shadow, to the mountains,
to the flowers, to the grass, to the fountains,
to the echo, to the air, to the winds
which carry away with them the sound of
   my futile words.
And if I don't have someone to hear me,
I talk about love to myself.

Voi, che sapete

from Act II
setting: near Seville, the 17th century; the palace of Count Almaviva; the Countess' apartment
character: Cherubino

After learning in Act I that he's bound for the army, Cherubino goes early in Act II to bewail this turn of events to the Countess Almaviva and Susanna in the Countess' boudoir. When Susanna asks him to sing one of his love songs for the Countess he is delighted. Susanna accompanies him on the guitar.

Voi, che sapete che cosa è amor,	*You ladies, who know what love is,*
donne, vedete, s'io l'ho nel cor.	*see if I have it in my heart.*
Quello ch'io provo, vi ridirò;	*What I feel, I'll repeat to you.*
è per me nuovo, capir nol so.	*It's new for me; I can't understand it.*
Sento un affetto pien di desir,	*I feel an emotion full of desire*
ch'ora è diletto, ch'ora è martir.	*which is now pleasure, now torture.*
Gelo, e poi sento l'alma	*I freeze, and then I feel my soul*
avvampar,	*bursting into flames;*
e in un momento torno a gelar.	*and in a moment I freeze again.*
Ricerco un bene fuori di me—	*I'm seeking a treasure outside of me—*
non so chi il tiene,	*I don't know who holds it;*
non so cos'è.	*I don't know what it is.*
Sospiro e gemo senza voler;	*I sigh and moan without wanting to;*
palpito e tremo senza saper.	*I quiver and tremble without knowing why.*
Non trovo pace notte nè dì,	*I find peace neither night nor day,*
ma pur mi piace languir così.	*but yet I enjoy languishing that way.*

COSÌ FAN TUTTE

(Women Are Like That)
1790
music by Wolfgang Amadeus Mozart
libretto by Lorenzo da Ponte

Smanie implacabili

from Act I, scene 3
setting: Naples, the 18th century; a drawing room in the house shared by the sisters Fiordiligi and Dorabella
character: Dorabella

Fiordiligi and Dorabella think that their soldier boyfriends, Ferrando and Gulglielmo, have just gone off to war. Dorabella, the younger of the two, melodramatically orders their maid, Despina, to close the shutters. Now that her lover is gone she prefers to remain alone and suffer.

Ah, scostati!	*Ah, stand aside!*
Paventa il tristo effetto	*Shun the dismal consequence*
d'un disperato affetto!	*of a despairing love!*
Chiudi quelle finestre—	*Close those windows—*
odio la luce,	*I hate the light,*
odio l'aria che spiro—	*I hate the air that I breathe—*
odio me stessa!	*I hate me myself!*
Chi schernisce il mio duol,	*Who is mocking my grief?*
chi mi consola?	*Who consoles me?*
Deh fuggi, per pietà;	*Ah, flee, for pity's sake;*
lasciami sola.	*leave me alone.*
Smanie implacabili	*Implacable frenzies*
che m'agitate,	*which agitate me,*
entro quest'anima	*within this soul*
più non cessate	*cease no more*
finchè l'angoscia	*until anguish*
mi fa morir.	*makes me die.*
Esempio misero	*A funereal example*
d'amor funesto	*of mournful love*
darò all'Eumenidi	*I will give to the Eumenides*
se viva resto	*if I remain alive*
col suono orribile	*with the horrible sound*
de' miei sospir.	*of my sighs.*

L'ITALIANA IN ALGERI

(The Italian Girl in Algiers)
1813
music by Gioachino Rossini
libretto by Angeli Anelli (originally for Luigi Mosca's 1808 opera of the same name)

Cruda sorte!... Già so per pratica

from Act I, scene 2
setting: a seashore in Algiers, c. 1800; a ship stranded on rocks after a violent storm
character: Isabella

Isabella, an Italian lady, finds herself shipwrecked on the Algerian shore. She was in search of her lost love, Lindoro, whose absence she laments. Ali, captain of Bey Mustafa's pirates, and his men seize the vessel and its passengers. The pirates look on with great joy in discovering so many new additions to the Bey's harem. Isabella, confident of her ability to handle any man, resolves to be fearless.

Cruda sorte! Amor tiranno!	*Cruel fate! Tyrannical love!*
Questo è il premio di mia fe':	*This is the reward of my faith:*
non v'è orror, terror,	*there is neither horror, terror,*
nè affanno	*nor anguish*
pari a quel ch'io provo in me.	*equal to that which I feel in me.*
Per te solo, o mio Lindoro,	*For you alone, oh my Lindoro,*
io mi trovo in tal periglio;	*I find myself in such peril;*
da chi spero, oh Dio! consiglio?	*from whom do I hope, oh God, for advice?*
Chi conforto mi darà?	*Who will give me comfort?*
Qua ci vuol disinvoltura;	*Here deftness is wanted;*
non più smanie, nè paura:	*no more frenzies or fear.*
di coraggio è tempo adesso...	*Now it's time for courage...*
or chi sono si vedrà.	*now they'll see who I am.*
Già so per pratica	*I already know through experience*
qual sia l'effetto	*what may be the effect*
d'un sguardo languido,	*of a languid glance,*
d'un sospiretto.	*of a little sigh.*
So a domar gli uomini come si fa,	*I know how men are tamed—*
sì, so a domar gli uomini come si fa.	*yes, I know how men are tamed.*
Sien dolci o ruvidi,	*Be they gentle or rough,*
sien flemma o foco,	*be they coolness or fire,*
son tutti simili a presso a poco.	*they are all the same, more or less.*
Tutti la chiedono,	*They all ask for it,*
tutti la bramano	*they all desire it:*
da vaga femmina felicità.	*happiness from a lovely woman.*
Sì sì...	*Yes, yes...*

IL BARBIERE DI SIVIGLIA

(The Barber of Seville)
1816
music by Gioachino Rossini
libretto by Cesare Sterbini (after *Le Barbier de Séville,* a comedy by Pierre Augustin Caron de Beaumarchais)

Una voce poco fa

from Act I, scene 2 (or Act II)
setting: Seville, the 17th century; a drawing room in the house of Dr. Bartolo
character: Rosina

Rosina is the ward of old Dr. Bartolo who plans to marry her. She, however, has fallen in love with a student, Lindoro, who is really the young Count Almaviva in disguise. He has been serenading her, and they have exchanged notes. Now, with another letter to Lindoro in her hand, she vows to foil Bartolo's plans and to follow her romantic longings.

Una voce poco fa	*A voice, a little while ago,*
qui nel cor mi risuonò;	*echoed here in my heart;*
il mio cor ferito è già,	*my heart is wounded now,*
e Lindor fu che il piagò.	*and it was Lindoro who covered it with wounds.*
Sì, Lindoro mio sarà,	*Yes, Lindoro will be mine—*
lo giurai, la vincerò.	*I've sworn it, I shall win.*
Il tutor ricuserà,	*My guardian will object.*
io l'ingegno aguzzerò;	*—I, quick-witted, will be sharp;*
alla fin s'accheterà,	*in the end he will acquiesce,*
e contenta io resterò.	*and I will be content.*
Io sono docile,	*I am submissive,*
son rispettosa,	*I'm respectful,*
sono ubbidiente,	*I'm obedient,*
dolce, amorosa;	*sweet, affectionate.*
mi lascio reggere,	*I allow myself to be governed;*
mi fo guidar.	*I let myself be guided.*
Ma se mi toccano	*But if they touch me*
dov'è il mio debole,	*where my sensitive spot is,*
sarò una vipera,	*I will be a viper,*
e cento trappole	*and I'll cause a hundred tricks*
prima di cedere farò giocar.	*to be played before giving in.*

LA CENERENTOLA

(Cinderella)
or *La Bontà in Trionfo (The Triumph of Goodness)*
1817
music by Gioachino Rossini
libretto by Jacopo Ferretti (after Charles Guillaume Etienne's libretto for *Cendrillon* by Nicolas Isouard, also after the fairy tale)

Non più mesta

from Act II
setting: Salerno, time unspecified (c. 18th century); a throne room in the palace of Don Ramiro
character: Angelina (Cenerentola)

In the final moments of this opera, after she is united in marriage to Prince Ramiro, Cenerentola gathers the bridal guests about her. She forgives all who have been cruel to her, including her father and her two stepsisters. The aria is an unusual and effective conclusion to the opera.

Nacqui all'affanno e al pianto.	*I was born to sorrow and weeping.*
Soffrì tacendo il core;	*My heart suffered silently;*
ma per soave incanto	*but through a kindly magic spell*
dell'età mia nel fiore,	*in the flower of my youth,*
come un baleno rapido	*swift as a bolt of lightning*
la sorte mia cangiò.	*my destiny changed.*
No, no, no, no:	*No, no, no, no:*
tergete il ciglio;	*dry your tears;*
perchè tremar?	*why tremble?*
A questo sen volate;	*Fly to this breast;*
figlia, sorella, amica—	*daughter, sister, friend—*
tutto trovate in me.	*find them all in me.*
Non più mesta accanto al fuoco	*No longer sad by the fire*
starò sola a gorgheggiar, no.	*will I remain alone, warbling—no.*
Ah fu un lampo, un sogno, un giuoco	*Ah, my long-time heartache was a flash,*
il mio lungo palpitar.	*a dream, a game.*

LUCREZIA BORGIA

1833
music by Gaetano Donizetti
libretto by Felice Romani (after the tragedy *Lucrèce Borgia* by Victor Hugo)

Il segreto per esser felici
(Brindisi)

from Act II
setting: Ferrara, the early 16th century; a banquet given by Lucrezia
character: Duke Orsini

The young Duke Orsini, at a party given by Lucrezia, wife of Don Alfonso, Duke of Ferrara, sings a rollicking drinking song, little knowing that the wine he quaffs has been poisoned by his hostess.

Il segreto per esser felici	*The secret for being happy*
so per prova	*I know through practice,*
e l'insegno agli amici.	*and I teach it to my friends.*
Sia sereno, sia nubilo il cielo,	*Whether the sky be clear or cloudy,*
ogni tempo, sia caldo, sia gelo,	*in every weather, be it hot or ice-cold,*
scherzo e bevo,	*I joke and drink,*
e derido gl'insani	*and I mock the madmen*
che si dan del futuro	*who devote themselves to thoughts*
pensier.	*of the future.*
Non curiamo l'incerto domani,	*We'll not care about the uncertain tomorrow,*
se quest'oggi n'è dato goder.	*if it's given to us to enjoy today.*
Profittiamo degl'anni fiorenti;	*Let's take advantage of the flowering years;*
il piacer li fa correr più lenti.	*pleasure makes them pass more slowly.*
Se vecchiezza con livida faccia	*If old age, with its grim face,*
stammi a tergo	*stands at my back*
e mia vita minaccia,	*and threatens my life,*
scherzo e bevo,	*I joke and drink,*
e derido gl'insani	*and I mock the madmen*
che si dan del futuro	*who devote themselves to thoughts*
pensier.	*of the future.*

LES HUGUENOTS

1836
music by Giacomo Meyerbeer
libretto by Eugène Scribe and Emile Deschamps (based on history)

Nobles seigneurs, salut!

from Act I
setting: Touraine, 1572; the banquet hall in the castle of Count de Nevers, a prominent Catholic party leader
character: Urbain

The Protestant nobleman, Raoul de Nangis, has been invited by the Count de Nevers to his home to meet his Catholic friends and to attempt a reconciliation between their parties. Urbain, the page of Marguerite de Valois, appears and greets the assembled nobles. His purpose is to escort Raoul, blindfolded, to an unspecified destination.

Nobles seigneurs, salut!	*Noble lords, greetings!*
Une dame noble et sage,	*A noble and virtuous lady,*
dont les rois seraient jaloux,	*of whom kings should be envious,*
m'a chargé de ce message,	*has entrusted me with this message*
chevaliers, pour l'un de vous,	*for one of you, chevaliers,*
sans qu'on la nomme,	*without my naming her;*
Honneur ici au gentilhomme	*honor here to the gentleman*
qu'elle a choisi!	*whom she has chosen!*

Vous pouvez croire	*You can believe*
que nul seigneur	*that no lord*
n'eut tant de gloire	*has ever had so much glory*
ni de bonheur, non, jamais!	*or good fortune—no, never!*
Ne craignez mensonge ou piège,	*Do not fear a lie or a trap,*
chevaliers, dans mes discours!	*chevaliers, in my speech!*
Or salut! Que Dieu protège	*Now farewell! May God protect*
vos combats, vos amours!	*your battles, your loves!*

LA FAVORITA

(The Favored Woman)
1840
music by Gaetano Donizetti
libretto by Alphonse Royer, Gustave Vaëz, and Eugène Scribe (after Baculard d'Arnaud's play *La Comte de Comminges*, and partly based on Eugène Scribe's libretto for *L'Ange de Nisida* by Donizetti)

O mio Fernando!

note: The original language of the opera is French, but an Italian translation has long been standard.
from Act III
setting: Castile, 1340; the palace of the Alcazar
character: Leonora

Leonora de Guzman, mistress of Alfonso XI, king of Castile, loves and is loved by Fernando, a monastic novice turned soldier. He seeks her hand from the king, not knowing her status, and the monarch finds it convenient to grant it. Leonora will sacrifice anything for Fernando's happiness, and determines to send him a letter telling him the truth.

Fia dunque vero, oh ciel?	*Can it be true then, oh heaven?*
Desso, Fernando, lo sposo di Leonora!	*He, Fernando, the husband of Leonora!*
Ah! Tutto mel dice,	*Ah! Everything tells me so,*
e dubbia è l'alma ancora	*and still my soul is uncertain*
all'inattesa gioia!	*at the unexpected joy!*
Oh Dio! Sposarlo?	*Oh God! To marry him?*
Oh mia vergogna estrema!	*Oh, my deepest shame!*
In dote al prode recar il disonor—	*To bring dishonor as dowry to the hero—*
no, mai;	*no, never;*
dovesse esecrarmi, fuggir,	*should he detest me and flee,*
saprà in brev'ora	*he will know soon*
chi sia la donna	*who the woman is*
che cotanto adora.	*whom he so much adores.*
O mio Fernando!	*Oh my Fernando!*
Della terra il trono a possederti	*To possess the throne of the country with you*
avria donato il cor;	*I would have given my heart;*
ma puro l'amor mio come il perdono,	*but my love, pure as your pardon,*
dannato, ahi lassa! è a	*is doomed—oh miserable me!—to*
disperato orror.	*desperate horror.*
Il ver fia noto,	*May the truth be known;*
e in tuo dispregio estremo,	*and in your deep contempt*
la pena avrommi	*I shall have the pain*
che maggior si de', ah!	*which must be the greatest—ah!*
Se il giusto tuo disdegno	*If your justified contempt*
allor fia scemo,	*still be wanting,*
piombi, gran Dio,	*may your thunderbolt,*
la folgor tua su me!	*great God, fall on me!*
Su, crudeli, e chi v'arresta?	*Come on, cruel ones—who is stopping you?*
Scritto è in cielo il mio dolor!	*My grief is written in heaven!*
Su, venite, ell'è una festa;	*Come on, come—it's a celebration;*
sparsa l'ara sia di fior.	*may the altar be strewn with flowers.*
Già la tomba a me s'appresta;	*Already the tomb readies itself for me;*
ricoperta in negro vel sia	*may the sad betrothed who, rejected and*
la trista fidanzata che reietta,	*despairing will not have forgiveness*
disperata, non avrà perdono in ciel.	*in heaven, be covered with a black veil.*

Maledetta, disperata, non avrà perdono in ciel.	Cursed, despairing, she will not have forgiveness in heaven.
Ah! crudeli, e chi v'arresta? Scritto in cielo è il mio dolor. Crudeli, venite.	Ah, cruel ones, who is stopping you? My grief is written in heaven. Cruel ones, come.
Ah! la trista fidanzata non avrà perdono in ciel.	Ah, the sad betrothed one will not have forgiveness in heaven.

IL TROVATORE
(The Troubadour)
1853
music by Giuseppe Verdi
libretto by Salvatore Cammarano, completed by Bardare at Cammarano's death in 1852 (after the play *El Trovador* by Antonio Garcia Gutiérrez)

Stride la vampa!

from Act II, scene 1
setting: Biscay, Spain, the 15th century; a gypsy camp in the mountains; early morning
character: Azucena

The gypsies have been singing a work song as they labor at their anvils by the fire. Their mood of contentment is shattered as the old gypsy Azucena dramatically recreates the story of how her mother was burned at the stake before a vengeful throng.

Stride la vampa! La folla indomita corre a quel foco lieta in sembianza! Urli di gioia intorno eccheggiano; cinta di sgherri donna s'avanza! Sinistra splende sui volti orribili la tetra fiamma che s'alza al ciel!	The blaze crackles! The indomitable crowd runs to that fire with happy faces! Screams of delight echo around; surrounded by ruffians a woman comes forward! Sinister shines on their horrible faces the ghastly flame that rises to the sky!
Stride la vampa! Giunge la vittima nero vestita, discinta e scalza! Grido feroce di morte levasi; l'eco il ripete di balza in balza!	The blaze crackles! The victim arrives dressed in black, ragged and barefoot! A fierce cry of death rises; the echo repeats it from cliff to cliff!

FAUST
1859
music by Charles Gounod
libretto by Jules Barbier and Michel Carré (after the drama by Johann Wolfgang von Goethe)

Faites-lui mes aveux

from Act III when played in 5 acts; Act II when played in four acts
setting: a village in Germany, the 16th century; a garden outside Marguerite's cottage
character: Siebel

The youth Siebel, in love with Marguerite, has vowed to protect her while her brother Valentin is away at war. Siebel pauses beside a bed of flowers, and begs the blossoms to carry his message of love to Marguerite.

Faites-lui mes aveux;	*Greet her for me;*
portez mes vœux!	*bear my wishes!*
Fleurs écloses près d'elle,	*Flowers in bloom close-by her,*
dites-lui qu'elle est belle,	*tell her that she is beautiful,*
que mon cœur nuit et jour	*that my heart night and day*
languit d'amour!	*languishes from love.*
Révélez à son âme	*Reveal to her soul*
le secret de ma flamme,	*the secret of my passion,*
qu'il s'exhale avec vous	*that it may give forth, with you,*
parfums plus doux!	*fragrances more sweet!*
Fanée! Hélas! ce sorcier,	*Withered! Alas, that sorcerer,*
que Dieu damne,	*whom God damns,*
m'a porté malheur!	*has brought me bad luck!*
Je ne puis, sans qu'elle se fane,	*I can't touch a flower*
toucher une fleur!	*without it withering!*
Si je trempais mes doigts	*Let me dip my fingers*
dans l'eau bénite!	*in the holy water!*
C'est là que chaque soir	*It's there that every evening*
vient prier Marguerite!	*Marguerite comes to pray!*
Voyons maintenant!	*Let's see now!*
Voyons vite!	*Let's see quickly!*
Elles se fanent?	*Are they withering?*
Non!	*No!*
Satan, je ris de toi!	*Satan, I laugh at you!*
C'est en vous que j'ai foi;	*It's in you that I have faith;*
parlez pour moi!	*speak for me!*
Qu'elle puisse connaître	*May she know*
l'émoi qu'elle a fait naître,	*the emotion she caused to be born,*
et dont mon cœur troublé	*and of which my troubled heart*
n'a point parlé!	*has not spoken at all!*
Si l'amour l'effarouche,	*If love startles her,*
que la fleur sur sa bouche	*may the flower upon her mouth*
sache au moins déposer	*at least be able to place*
un doux baiser!	*a sweet kiss!*

ROMÉO ET JULIETTE

(Romeo and Juliet)
1867
music by Charles Gounod
libretto by Jules Barbier and Michel Carré (after the tragedy by William Shakespeare)

Que fais-tu, blanche tourterelle

from Act III, scene 2
setting: Verona, the 14th century; a square outside the Capulet palace
character: Stephano

Stephano, Romeo's page, wanders into the square in front of the Capulet palace looking for his master whom he has not seen since the previous day. He fears that Romeo may be held captive by the Capulets. The page sings a mocking serenade about a turtle dove in a nest of vultures.

Depuis hier je cherche en vain	*Since yesterday I've been searching in vain*
mon maître!	*for my master!*
Est-il encore chez vous,	*Is he still at your house,*
Messeigneurs Capulet?	*my lords Capulet?*
Voyons un peu si vos dignes valets	*Well now, let's see if your worthy servants*
à ma voix ce matin oseront	*will dare to reappear this morning*
reparaître!	*at my voice!*
Que fais-tu, blanche tourterelle,	*What are you doing, white turtledove,*
dans ce nid de vautours?	*in that nest of vultures?*
Quelque jour, déployant ton aîle,	*One day, spreading your wings,*
tu suivras les amours!	*you will follow love!*

Aux vautours il faut la bataille;	To vultures battle is necessary;
pour frapper d'estoc et de taille	to thrust and cut
leurs becs sont aiguisés!	their beaks are whetted.
Laisse là ces oiseaux de proie,	Leave those birds of prey there,
tourterelle, qui fais ta joie	turtledove, who find your joy
des amoureux baisers!	in amorous kisses!
Gardez bien la belle!	Guard the beautiful girl well!
Qui vivra verra!	Time will tell!
Votre tourterelle vous échappera!	Your turtledove will escape from you!

Un ramier, loin du vert bocage,	A wood-pigeon, far from the green grove,
par l'amour attiré,	allured by love,
à l'entour de ce nid sauvage	around that savage nest
a, je crois, soupiré!	has, I believe, sighed!
Les vautours sont à la curée;	The vultures are at the spoils;
leurs chansons que fuit Cythérée	their songs, which Cytherea flees,
résonnent à grand bruit!	resound boisterously!
Cependant, en leur douce ivresse,	Meanwhile, in their sweet ecstasy
nos amants content leur tendresse	our lovers recount their tenderness
aux astres de la nuit!	to the stars of the night!

DIE FLEDERMAUS

(The Bat)
1874
music by Johann Strauss, Jr.
libretto by Carl Haffner and Richard Genée (after the comedy *Le Réveillon* by Henri Meilhac and Ludovic Halévy, which itself was based on the comedy *Das Gefängnis* by Roderich Benedix)

Chacun à son goût

from Act II
setting: Vienna, the 19th century; a ballroom; a party hosted by the Russian Prince Orlofsky
character: Prince Orlofsky

In this favorite Viennese operetta the epicene Prince Orlofsky is giving a glorious party. He declares his hedonistic philosophy in this strophic air.

Ich lade gern mir Gäste ein;	I enjoy inviting guests over;
man lebt bei mir recht fein.	they have a truly grand time at my house.
Man unterhält sich wie man mag,	They chat with each other as people will,
oft bis zum hellen Tag.	often up until the light of day.
Zwar langweil' ich mich stets dabei,	In truth, I'm always bored with
was man auch treibt und spricht;	what they do and say;
indess, was mir als Wirt steht frei,	meanwhile, what I am free to be as host
duld' ich bei Gästen nicht.	I don't endure among the guests.

Und sehe ich, es ennüyiert sich	And if I see that someone is getting bored
jemand hier bei mir,	here at my house,
so pack' ich ihn ganz ungeniert—	then I send him off quite unabashedly—
werf ihn hinaus zur Tür.	I throw him out the door.

Und fragen Sie, ich bitte,	And should you ask, if you please,
warum ich das denn tu?	why I do that,
'sist mal bei mir so Sitte:	it's just the custom at my house:
chacun à son goût!	each to his own taste!

Wenn ich mit andern sitz' beim Wein	Whenever I sit with others by the wine
und Flasch' um Flasche leer',	and empty bottle after bottle,
muß jeder mit mir durstig sein,	everyone has to be thirsty with me,
sonst werde grob ich sehr.	or else I become very uncivil.

Und schenke Glas um Glas ich ein,	*And as I fill glass after glass*

Und schenke Glas um Glas ich ein,
duld' ich nicht Widerspruch;
nicht leiden kann ich's,
wenn sie schrein:
ich will nicht, hab' genug!

And as I fill glass after glass
I don't endure opposition;
I can't bear it
when they cry,
"I don't want to—I've had enough!"

Wer mir beim Trinken nicht pariert,
sich zieret wie ein Tropf,
dem werfe ich ganz ungeniert
die Flasche an den Kopf.

Whoever doesn't equal me in drinking,
politely refuses like a ninny—
I'll quite unabashedly toss
the bottle at his head.

CARMEN

1875
music by Georges Bizet
libretto by Henri Meilhac and Ludovic Halévy (after the novel by Prosper Mérimée)

L'amour est un oiseau rebelle
(Habañera)

from Act I
setting: Seville, c. 1820; a public square outside a tobacco factory
character: Carmen

Men wait outside the tobacco factory to see the working women on their break. They are disappointed that the alluring gypsy, Carmen, is not among them. When she finally appears she sings the famous "Habañera."

L'amour est un oiseau rebelle
que nul ne peut apprivoiser,
et c'est bien en vain
qu'on l'appelle,
s'il lui convient de refuser!
Rien n'y fait,
menace ou prière—
l'un parle bien,
l'autre se tait;
et c'est l'autre
que je préfère—
il n'a rien dit,
mais il me plaît.
L'amour!

Love is a rebellious bird
that no one can tame;
and it's truly in vain
that one call him,
if it suits him to refuse!
Nothing helps—
threat nor entreaty.
The one man speaks well,
the other keeps quiet;
and it's the other
whom I prefer—
he hasn't said anything,
but he pleases me.
Love!

L'amour est enfant de Bohême;
il n'a jamais connu de loi.
Si tu ne m'aimes pas,
je t'aime;
mais si je t'aime,
prends garde à toi!

Love is a bohemian child;
he has never known law.
If you don't love me,
I love you;
but if I love you,
watch out for yourself!

L'oiseau que tu croyais surprendre
battit de l'aile et s'envola.
L'amour est loin—
tu peux l'attendre;
tu ne l'attends plus,
il est là!
Tout autour de toi,
vite, il vient, s'en va,
puis il revient.
Tu crois le tenir,
il t'évite;
tu crois l'éviter,
il te tient!
L'amour!

The bird that you thought to catch
flapped his wings and flew away.
Love is far away—
you may wait for it;
when you don't wait anymore,
there it is!
All around you,
quickly it comes, goes away;
then it comes back again.
When you think you have hold of it,
it evades you;
when you think you're evading it,
it has hold of you!
Love!

Près des remparts de Séville
(Seguidilla)

from Act I
setting: Seville, c. 1820; a public square outside a tobacco factory
character: Carmen

After a fight in the tobacco factory, Carmen is arrested. Left under the surveillance of Don José, a corporal in the dragoons, she flirts with him, hoping that he will help her to escape. She tells him that a flower that she gave to him earlier has enchanted him and that he is now hopelessly in love with her. With her hands tied, she sways in the insinuating rhythm of the Seguidilla, inviting him to run away with her to the inn of Lillas Pastia outside the city.

Près des remparts de Séville,	*Near the ramparts of Seville,*
chez mon ami Lillas Pastia,	*at my friend Lillas Pastia's*
j'irai danser la Séguédille	*I will go to dance the seguidilla,*
et boire du manzanilla.	*and to drink manzanilla.*
J'irai chez mon ami Lillas Pastia.	*I will go to my friend Lillas Pastia's.*
Oui, mais toute seule on s'ennuie,	*Yes—but all alone one is bored,*
et les vrais plaisirs sont à deux;	*and true pleasures are with another person;*
donc, pour me tenir compagnie,	*so, to keep me company,*
j'emmènerai mon amoureux!	*I'll take along my lover!*
Mon amoureux!... il est au diable!	*My lover... he belongs to the devil!*
Je l'ai mis à la porte hier!	*I threw him out yesterday!*
Mon pauvre cœur, très consolable,	*My poor heart, very consolable,*
est libre comme l'air!	*is free as the breeze!*
J'ai des galants à la douzaine,	*I have suitors by the dozen,*
mais ils ne sont pas à mon gré.	*but they are not to my liking.*
Voici la fin de la semaine:	*Here is the end of the week:*
Qui veut m'aimer? Je l'aimerai!	*Who wishes to love me? I will love him!*
Qui veut mon âme? Elle est à prendre!	*Who wants my soul? It is to be had!*
Vous arrivez au bon moment!	*You come at the right moment!*
Je n'ai guère le temps d'attendre,	*I haven't the time to wait,*
car avec mon nouvel amant	*for with my new lover*
près des remparts de Séville,	*near the ramparts of Seville*
nous danserons la Séguédille	*we will dance the seguidilla*
et boirons du manzanilla:	*and we'll drink manzanilla:*
tra la la...	*tra la la!...*

En vain, pour éviter

from Act III
setting: the mountains near the Spanish border, c. 1820; night
character: Carmen

In a wild mountain glen the gypsies rest during their smuggling operation. Carmen's friends, Frasquita and Mercédes, have just told their own fortunes in the cards. Carmen, in another part of the clearing, spreads out her cards again and again, only to reveal the same fate: death... first for Don José and then for herself.

Voyons, que j'essaie à mon tour.	*Let's see—let me try my turn.*
Carreau! Pique!	*Diamonds! Spades!*
La mort! J'ai bien lu—	*Death! I've read correctly—*
moi d'abord, ensuite lui—	*me first, then him—*
pour tous les deux, la mort!	*for both of us, death!*
En vain, pour éviter les réponses amères,	*In vain, to avoid the bitter answers,*
tu mêleras!	*you will shuffle!*
Cela ne sert à rien;	*That is of no use;*
les cartes sont sincères	*the cards are truthful*
et ne mentiront pas!	*and will not lie!*
Dans le livre d'en haut	*In the book on high*
si ta page est heureuse,	*if your page is auspicious,*
mêle et coupe sans peur:	*shuffle and cut without fear:*
la carte sous tes doigts	*the card beneath your fingers*
se tournera joyeuse,	*will turn up joyful,*
t'annonçant le bonheur!	*foretelling good fortune!*

Mais si tu dois mourir—	*But if you must die—*
si le mot redoutable	*if the terrible word*
est écrit par le sort—	*is written by fate—*
recommence vingt fois,	*even if you begin again twenty times,*
la carte impitoyable	*the unrelenting card*
répétera: la mort!	*will repeat: death!*
Oui, si tu dois mourir,	*Yes, if you must die,*
recommence vingt fois,	*even if you begin again twenty times,*
la carte impitoyable	*the unrelenting card*
répétera: la mort	*will repeat: death!*
Encor!	*Again!*
Toujours la mort!	*Always death!*

LA GIOCONDA

(The Cheerful Girl)
1876
music by Amilcare Ponchielli
libretto by "Tobia Gorria," a pseudonym for Arrigo Boito (after *Angelo, Tyran de Padoue* by Victor Hugo)

Voce di donna

from Act I
setting: Venice, the 17th century; the courtyard of the ducal palace, decorated for a holiday festival; a spring afternoon
character: La Cieca

La Cieca, the blind mother of the Venetian street singer Gioconda, is wrongfully accused of witchcraft. Laura, the wife of Alvise, a chief of State Inquisition, intervenes on her behalf. In this aria La Cieca bestows upon Laura her rosary and her thanks.

Voce di donna o d'angelo	*The voice of a woman or an angel*
le mie catene ha sciolto;	*has loosened my fetters.*
mi vietan le mie tenebre	*My blindness keeps me from*
di quella santa il volto,	*the sight of that saintly one;*
pure da me non partasi	*yet may she not part from me*
senza un pietoso don, no!	*without a pious gift—no!*
A te questo rosario	*To you this rosary,*
che le preghiere aduna.	*which assembles the prayers.*
Io te lo porgo—	*I offer it to you—*
accettalo;	*accept it;*
ti porterà fortuna.	*it will bring you good fortune.*
Sulla tua testa vigili	*May my blessing watch over*
la mia benedizion.	*your head.*

SAMSON ET DALILA

(Samson and Delilah)
1877
music by Camille Saint-Saëns
libretto by Ferdinand Lemaire (after the Old Testament, Judges xiv-xvi)

Printemps qui commence

from Act I
setting: Gaza, Palestine, 1136 B.C.; a public square
character: Dalila

Samson has led the Hebrews to victory over the Philistines. Dalila and other priestesses of the Temple of Dagon pay tribute to the warrior and seductively dance around him. Dalila invites him to the flower-scented valley of Sorek, saying that she will wait for him there.

Printemps qui commence,	*Spring, which begins,*
portant l'espérance	*bringing hope*
aux cœurs amoureux,	*to loving hearts,*
ton souffle qui passe	*your passing breath*
de la terre efface	*erases from the earth*
les jours malheureux.	*the unhappy days.*
Tout brûle en notre âme,	*Everything is on fire in our souls,*
et ta douce flamme	*and your sweet flame*
vient sécher nos pleurs;	*comes to dry our tears;*
tu rends à la terre,	*you restore to the earth,*
par un doux mystère,	*by a sweet mystery,*
les fruits et les fleurs.	*the fruits and the flowers.*
En vain je suis belle!	*In vain I am beautiful!*
Mon cœur plein d'amour,	*My heart, full of love,*
pleurant l'infidèle,	*weeping for the unfaithful one,*
attend son retour!	*awaits his return!*
Vivant d'espérance,	*Living in hope,*
mon cœur désolé	*my desolate heart*
garde souvenance	*cherishes the memory*
du bonheur passé!	*of past happiness!*
A la nuit tombante	*At nightfall*
j'irai, triste amante,	*I will go, a dejected lover,*
m'asseoir au torrent,	*to sit by the stream—*
l'attendre en pleurant!	*to await him, weeping!*
Chassant ma tristesse,	*Casting off my sadness,*
s'il revient un jour,	*if he returns one day,*
à lui ma tendresse	*his is my tenderness*
et la douce ivresse	*and the sweet ecstasy*
qu'un brûlant amour	*which a burning love*
garde à son retour!	*keeps for his return!*

Amour! viens aider ma faiblesse!

from Act II
setting: the valley of Sorek, Palestine, 1136 B.C.: Dalila's house, surrounded by a tropical garden
character: Dalila

Dalila awaits Samson's arrival. She invokes the god of love to aid her in destroying the arch-enemy of her people.

Samson, recherchant ma présence,	*Samson, desiring my presence,*
ce soir doit venir en ces lieux.	*must come to this place tonight.*
Voici l'heure de la vengeance	*The hour of vengeance, which must*
qui doit satisfaire nos dieux!	* satisfy our gods, is here!*
Amour! viens aider ma faiblesse!	*Love, come to aid my weakness!*
Verse le poison dans son sein!	*Pour the poison into his bosom!*
Fais que, vaincu par mon adresse,	*Make Samson, vanquished by my skill,*
Samson soit enchaîné demain!	* be bound in chains tomorrow!*
Il voudrait en vain de son âme	*In vain should he wish to be able to*
pouvoir me chasser, me bannir!	* drive me out, banish me, from his soul!*
Pourrait-il éteindre la flamme	*Could he be able to quench the flame*
qu'alimente le souvenir?	*which memory feeds?*
Il est à moi! C'est mon esclave!	*He is mine! He is my slave!*
Mes frères craignent son courroux;	*My brethren fear his wrath;*
moi seule, entre tous, je le brave,	*I alone, among all—I defy him,*
et le retiens à mes genoux!	*and restrain him at my knees!*
Contre l'amour, sa force est vaine;	*Against love, his strength is in vain;*
et lui, le fort parmi les forts—	*and he, the strongest among the strong—*
lui, qui d'un peuple rompt la chaîne,	*he, who breaks a peoples' chains,*
succombera sous mes efforts!	*will yield under my endeavors!*

Mon cœur s'ouvre à ta voix

from Act II
setting: the valley of Sorek, Palestine, 1136 B.C.; Dalila's house, surrounded by a tropical garden; night
character: Dalila

Samson comes to see Dalila. He tries to resist her embrace as a storm that reflects the turbulence in his heart breaks outside. Finally he cries that destiny has decreed this fatal attraction. Dalila responds with this seductive, passionate aria which concludes with Samson's declaration of love.

Mon cœur s'ouvre à ta voix	*My heart opens up at your voice*
comme s'ouvrent les fleurs	*as the flowers open up*
aux baisers de l'aurore!	*at the kisses of dawn!*
Mais, ô mon bien-aimé,	*But, oh my beloved,*
pour mieux sécher mes pleurs,	*so as better to dry my tears,*
que ta voix parle encore!	*may your voice speak again!*
Dis-moi qu'à Dalila tu reviens	*Tell me that you return to Dalila*
pour jamais;	*forever;*
redis à ma tendresse	*repeat to my tender love*
les serments d'autrefois—	*the promises of former times—*
ces serments que j'aimais!	*those promises that I loved!*
Ah! réponds à ma tendresse!	*Ah, respond to my tenderness!*
Verse-moi l'ivresse!	*Fill me with ecstasy!*
Ainsi qu'on voit des blés	*Just as one sees the stalks*
les épis onduler	*of wheat undulate*
sous la brise légère,	*beneath the gentle breeze,*
ainsi frémit mon cœur,	*so my heart quivers,*
prêt à se consoler	*ready to be consoled*
à ta voix qui m'est chère!	*at your voice that is dear to me!*
La flèche est moins rapide	*The arrow is less quick*
à porter le trépas	*to bring death*
que ne l'est ton amante	*than your lover is*
à voler dans tes bras!	*to fly into your arms!*
Samson! je t'aime!	*Samson, I love you!*

CAVALLERIA RUSTICANA
(Rustic Chivalry)
1890
music by Pietro Mascagni
libretto by Giovanni Targioni-Tozzetti and Guido Menasci (after a story by Giovanni Verga)

Voi lo sapete

in one act
setting: a Sicilian village, the 19th century; a village square outside a church; Easter morning
character: Santuzza

Townsfolk have entered the church for Easter Sunday services. Mamma Lucia, keeper of a wineshop, and Santuzza, a village girl, are left in the piazza. Santuzza tells Lucia of her desperate passion for the woman's son, Turridu, who has thrown her aside for his old love, Lola, wife of Alfio.

Voi lo sapete, o mamma:	*You know it, oh mamma:*
prima d'andar soldato	*before going away as a soldier*
Turiddu aveva a Lola	*Turiddu had sworn*
eterna fè giurato.	*eternal faith to Lola.*
Tornò, la seppe sposa;	*When he returned, he learned she was married;*
e con un nuovo amore	*and with a new love*
volle spegner la fiamma	*he wanted to extinguish the flame*
che gli bruciava il core.	*that burned his heart.*
M'amò. L'amai. Ah!	*He loved me. I loved him. Ah!*
Quell'invida	*That woman, envious*
d'ogni delizia mia,	*of my every delight,*
del suo sposo dimentica.	*forgets her husband.*
Arse di gelosia;	*She burned with jealousy;*
me l'ha rapito!	*she took him away from me!*
Priva dell'onor mio rimango.	*I am left deprived of my honor.*
Lola e Turiddu s'amano;	*Lola and Turiddu love each other;*
io piango.	*I weep.*
Io son dannata.	*I am damned.*

WERTHER

1892
music by Jules Massenet
libretto by Edouard Blau, Georges Hartmann and Paul Milliet (after the novel *Die Leiden des jungen Werther* by Johann Wolfgang von Goethe)

Va! laisse couler mes larmes

from Act III
setting: near Frankfurt, c. 1780; the parlor in the home of Albert and Charlotte; Christmas
character: Charlotte

The young Werther is in love with Charlotte. Though she returned that love, she felt bound to marry Werther's friend Albert. Werther has gone away, but he continues to write to Charlotte. Re-reading his letters, she realizes that she still loves him. When her sister Sophie, in trying to cheer her, mentions Werther's name, Charlotte bursts into tears.

Va! laisse couler mes larmes—	*Go! Let my tears flow—*
elles font du bien, ma chérie!	*they do me good, my dear!*
Les larmes qu'on ne pleure pas	*The tears that people do not shed*
dans notre âme retombent toutes,	*all sink into our souls,*
et de leurs patientes gouttes	*and with their steady drops*
martèlent le cœur triste et las!	*hammer the sad and weary heart!*
Sa résistance enfin s'épuise;	*Its resistance is finally exhausted;*
le cœur se creuse et s'affaiblit:	*the heart becomes hollow and grows weak:*
il est trop grand, rien ne l'emplit;	*it is too big—nothing will fill it up;*
et trop fragile, tout le brise!	*and too fragile—anything will break it!*

ADRIANA LECOUVREUR
1902
music by Francesco Cilea
libretto by Arturo Colautti (after the play by Eugène Scribe and Gabriel Jean Baptiste Legouvé)

Acerba voluttà

from Act II
setting: Paris, 1730
character: La Principessa (Princesse de Bouillon)

In eighteenth century Paris the Princesse de Bouillon is the rival of Adriana Lecouvreur, the star of the Comédie Française, for the love of Maurice de Sax. In this soliloquy which opens Act II she nervously awaits the arrival of Maurice for an assignation.

Acerba voluttà, dolce tortura,
   lentissima agonia, rapida offesa,
   vampa, gelo, tremor, smania, paura,
   ad amoroso sen torna l'attesa!
Ogni eco, ogni ombra nella notte incesa
contro la impaziente alma congiura:
fra dubbiezza e desìo tutta sospesa,
l'eternità nell'attimo misura.
Verrà? M'oblia?
S'affretta?
O pur si pente?
Ecco, egli giunge!
No, del fiume è il verso,
misto al sospir d'un arbore dormente.
O vagabonda stella d'Oriente,
non tramontar;
sorridi all'universo,
e s'egli non mente,
scorta il mio amor!

Waiting brings back intense pleasure, sweet
*   torment, enduring pain, quick offense,*
*   fire, ice, trembling, rage, and fear*
*   to my loving breast!*
Every echo, every shadow in the incandescent night
conspires against my impatient soul:
completely suspended between doubt and desire,
it measures eternity in the moment.
Will he come? Has he forgotten me?
Is he hurrying?
Or perhaps he is changing his mind?
There, he's coming!
No, it's the sound of the stream,
mingled with the sigh of a sleeping tree.
Oh vagrant star of the east,
do not wane;
smile at the universe
and, if he is not lying,
guide my love!

THE MOTHER OF US ALL
1947
music by Virgil Thomson
libretto by Gertrude Stein (scenario by Maurice Grosser)

We cannot retrace our steps

from Act II, scene 3
setting: 19th century America; the Congressional Hall
character: Susan B. Anthony

In the final scene of this unusual opera there is an unveiling ceremony for a statue of Susan B. Anthony. The festivities get out of hand, but finally the statue is unveiled. Susan B. herself, regally dressed, is on the pedestal. The guests leave, and she reflects on her long life in semi-darkness to an empty stage.

THE CONSUL
1950
music and libretto by Gian Carlo Menotti

Lullaby

from Act II, scene 1
setting: a large city in a police state somewhere in Europe, post World War II; a small, shabby apartment shared by John and Magda Sorel, their baby, and John's mother; evening
character: the Mother

John Sorel, a political activist, has fled to the border, hounded by the secret police. He will cross it when his family can join him. Magda, his wife, tries desperately to secure visas for herself, her baby boy, and John's mother but encounters endless red tape. This is the lullaby which the Mother sings to her tiny grandson, who is seriously ill from hunger and cold.

THE SAINT OF BLEECKER STREET
1954
music and libretto by Gian Carlo Menotti

Ah, Michele, don't you know

from Act II
setting: an Italian neighborhood in New York City, the present (1954); an Italian restaurant in the basement of a house on Bleecker Street
character: Desideria

Annina is a passionate religious mystic who experiences stigmata. Her brother Michele, though an agnostic, is devoted to her. Spurned by the Catholic community, his worldly-minded girlfriend, Desideria, cries out for his love and then taunts him by accusing him of saving that love for his sister.

THE BALLAD OF BABY DOE
1956
music by Douglas Moore
libretto by John Latouche (based on the life of Baby Doe Tabor, 1854-1935)

Augusta! How can you turn away?

from Act II, scene 4
setting: Leadville, Colorado, 1896; Augusta's parlor; November
character: Augusta Tabor

Horace Tabor, the silver king of Colorado, left his wife Augusta for the young and lovely Baby Doe. Now the value of silver has plummeted, leaving Horace destitute. Baby Doe's mother, Mama McCourt, comes to Augusta to plead for financial help for Horace (unbeknownst to him). Though moved, Augusta asks her to leave her in peace. Alone, Augusta reflects on her past life with Horace and the bitterness that remains.

VANESSA
1958
music by Samuel Barber
libretto by Gian Carlo Menotti

Must the winter come so soon?

from Act I, scene 1
setting: a northern country, c. 1905; a drawing room in Vanessa's country house; a night in early winter
character: Erika

At her remote and elegant country estate the beautiful Vanessa, abandoned by her lover Anatol twenty years before, awaits his return, heralded by a letter. Erika, her niece, wonders if the carriage sent to bring their visitor will be able to return through the swirling snows of an early winter storm.

When I am laid in earth

from
DIDO AND AENEAS

Henry Purcell

When I am laid,＿ am laid ＿ in earth, may my wrongs ＿ cre - ate No trou - ble, no trou -ble in thy breast. When I am laid,＿ am laid ＿ in

mem - ber me, but ah! for - get my

fate.

Che farò senza Euridice?

from
ORFEO ED EURIDICE

Christoph Willibald von Gluck

di - ce!   Con - sor - te!

Ah, più non vi - ve! La chia - mo in - van.

Mi - se - ro me, la per - do e di nuo - vo e per sempre! Oh

leg - ge! Oh mor - te! Oh ri - cor - do cru - del! Non ho soc -

* Appoggiatura possible

32

cor - so, non m'a-van - za con - si - glio. Io veg-go so - lo (Oh___

___ fie-ra vi-sta!) il lut-tu-o-so a-spet-to dell' or-ri-do mio sta-to!

Sa-zia-ti, sor-te re-a: son di-spe-ra-to!

Allegretto

Che fa - rò sen-za Eu - ri - di - ce? Do-ve an- drò sen-za il mio

ben? Che__ fa - rò?_____ Do - ve an - drò?_____ Che__ fa -

rò__ sen - za il mi-o ben? Do - ve an - drò__ sen - za il mi-o

ben? Eu - ri - di - ce! Eu - ri - di - ce! Oh

Non so più cosa son

from
LE NOZZE DI FIGARO

Wolfgang Amadeus Mozart

Allegro vivace

CHERUBINO:

Non so più co-sa son, co-sa fac - cio; or di

fo - co,o-ra so - no di ghiac - cio. O-gni don - na can-giar di co-

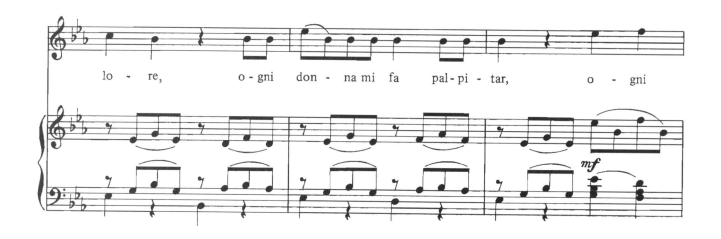

lo - re, o-gni don - na mi fa pal-pi - tar, o - gni

donna mi_ fa palpitar, ogni donna mi fa palpitar. So_ lo ai nomi d'amor, di di letto, mi si turba, mi s'altera il petto, e a parlare mi_ sforza d'amore

un de - si - o,   un   de - si - o ch'io non

pos - so spie - gar, un de - si - o,   un   de -

si - o ch'io non   pos - so   spie - gar._____   Non so

piu co - sa son, co - sa fac - cio;   or di fo - co,o - ra so - no di

ghiac - cio. O-gni don - na can-giar di co - lo - re, o - gni

don - na mi fa pal-pi - tar, o - gni don - na mi

fa pal - pi - tar, o - gni don - na mi fa pal - pi -

tar. Par - lo d'a-mor ve -

glian - do,   par - lo d'a-mor so -

gnan - do,   all' ac - qua, all'om - bra, ai mon - ti,   ai fio - ri, all' er - be, ai

fp

fp

f   p

fon - ti,   all' e - co, all' a - ria, ai ven - ti,   che il suon de' va - ni ac -

cen - ti,____ por - ta - no via con   se,____ por - ta - no

cresc.   f   colla voce   p

via con se. Par - lo d'a-mor ve - glian - do,

par - lo d'a-mor so - gnan - do, all' ac - qua, all' om - bra,

ai mon - ti, ai fio - ri, all' er - be, ai fon - ti, all'

e - co, all'a - ria, ai ven - ti, che il suon de' va - ni ac - cen - ti,

cresc.   f   p   cresc.

44

por - ta - no via con se,_____ por - ta - no via con

se._____ E se non ho chi m'o - da, e

Adagio

se non ho chi m'o - da, par - lo d'a-mor con

Tempo I

me,_____ con me,_____ par - lo d'a-mor con me.

*Appoggiaturas are optional here.

Voi, che sapete

from
LE NOZZE DI FIGARO

Wolfgang Amadeus Mozart

don - ne, ve-de-te,___ s'io l'ho___ nel___ cor.

Quel - lo ch'io pro - vo, vi___ ri - di - rò;___

è per me nuo - vo, ca - pir nol so.

Sen - to un af - fet - to pien di de - sir,___

ch'o - ra è di - let - to, ch'o - ra è mar - tir.

Ge - lo,e poi sen - to l'al - ma av - vam - par,

e in un mo - men - to___ tor - no a ge - lar.

Ri - cer-co un be - ne fuo - ri di me___

non so chi il tie - ne, non so cos' - è. So-spi-ro e

ge - mo sen - za vo - ler; pal - pi-to e tre - mo sen - za sa -

per. Non tro-vo pa - ce not - te nè dì, ma pur mi pia - ce

lan - guir co - sì. Voi, che sa - pe - te

che co - sa è a - mor, don - ne, ve - de - te,

s'io l'ho nel cor, don - ne, ve - de - te,____

s'io l'ho nel cor, don - ne, ve - de - te,____

s'io l'ho__ nel__ cor.

Smanie implacabili

from
COSÌ FAN TUTTE

Wolfgang Amadeus Mozart

* Appoggiatura possible

ca - bi - li che m'a - gi - ta - te, en - tro quest'a - ni - ma

più non ces - sa - te fin - chè l'an - go - scia mi fa mo -

rir, mi fa mo - rir. E -

sem - pio mi - se - ro d'a - mor fu -

spir.

Sma - nie im - pla -

cresc. *f* *p*

ca - bi - li_____ che m'a - gi - ta - te, en - tro quest'

a - ni - ma_____ più non ces - sa - te fin - chè l'an -

go - scia mi fa mo - rir, mi__ fa mo -

mfp

Cruda sorte!... Già so per pratica

from
L'ITALIANA IN ALGERI

Giachino Rossini

Cru - da sor - te! A - mor ti - ran - no! Que - sto è il

pre - mi - o di mi - a fe': non v'è or - ror, ter - ror, nè af -

fan - no pa - ri a quel ch'io pro - vo in me. Per te

solo, o mio Lin-do-ro, i-o mi tro-vo in tal _____ pe-

ri - glio; da chi spe - ro, oh Di-o! con-si - glio, oh Di-o! con-

si - glio? Chi con-for - to __ mi da - rà? Da chi

spe - ro, oh_ Di-o! con-si - glio? Chi con-for - to ___ mi ___ da -

non più sma-nie, **né** pa - u - ra: di co-rag-gio è tem-po a-

des - so... or chi so - no si ve-drà, or chi

so - no si ve - drà. Già_so per

pra - ti - ca qual_sia l'ef - fet - to d'un sguar-do lan - gui-do, d'un_so-spi-

ret - to. So a do-mar gli uo-mi - ni co - me si fa, sì, sì, sì,

sì. So a do-mar gli uo - mi - ni co - me si fa, sì, so a do - mar

gli uo-mi - ni co - me si_ fa. Sien dol - ci o

ru - vi-di, sien flem-ma o fo - co, son tut - ti

64

tà,____ fe - li - ci - tà,____ fe - li - ci - tà, da va - ga

fem-mi-na fe - li ____ ci ____ ta, da va - ga fem-mi-na fe - li - ci -

tà, fe - li - ci - tà,____ fe - li - ci -

tà, fe - li - ci - tà.

Una voce poco fa

from
IL BARBIERE DI SIVIGLIA

Gioachino Rossini

rà,   lo giu - ra - i,   la __ vin - ce - rò.

Il tu - tor ri - cu - se - rà,   io l'in - ge - gno a - guz - ze -

rò;   al - la fin s'ac - che - te - rà,   e con - ten - ta io re - ste -

rò.   Sì, Lin - do - ro __ mi - o sa - rà,   lo __ giu -

ra - i, la — vin - ce - rò. Sì, Lin - do - ro — mi - o — sa -

rà, lo giu - ra - i, la vin - ce - rò!

do - ci-le, so-no ub-bi-

dien-te, mi la-scio reg-ge-re, mi fo gui-dar. _____

_____ Ma se mi toc - ca-no do-v'è il mio de - bo-le, sa-rò u-na

vi - pe - ra, _____ sa - rò, e cen-to trap-po-le pri-ma di

ce - de-re fa-rò gio - car,___ fa - rò___ gio - car, e cen-to

trap - po-le pri-ma di ce - de-re fa-rò gio - car,___ fa - rò___ gio -

col canto *a tempo*

car, e___ cen-to___ trap - po-le pri-ma_di_ce - de-re, e cen-to

col canto *a tempo*

a piacere

trap-po - le fa - rò, fa - rò gio - car, e cen-to

f

trap-po-le fa - rò gio - car, e___ cen - to trap-po-le fa-rò gio -

car, fa - rò gio - car, fa - rò gio -

[ten.]

car,___ fa - rò gio - car.

[colla voce] f

ff

Non più mesta

from
LA CENERENTOLA

Gioachino Rossini

ANGELINA:

Nac - qui al - l'af - fan - no e al

pian - to. Sof - frì_____ ta - cen - do il

col canto

pp

co - - re;

ma per so - a - ve____ in_ can - - to

cresc.

dell' e - tà mi - a____ nel__ fio - - re,

co - me un ba - le - - no_____

ra - pi-do la sor-te mi - a, la__ sor-te mi - a can -

giò, co - me un ba - le - no_____

ra - - pi-do la sor-te mi-a, la__ sor-te mi-a can -

fuo - co sta - rò so - la a_ gor - gheg - giar, no. Ah fu_un lam - po,un so - gno, un giuo - co il mi - o lun - go_____ pal - pi - tar. Non più me - sta ac-can - to al fuo - co, non più me - sta ac-can - to al fuo - co_sta - rò

so - la a_ gor - gheg - giar, no. Ah fu un lam - po, un so - gno, un

giuo - co, il mio lun - go____ pal - pi -

tar. Non più me - sta ac - can - to al

fuo - co. non più me - sta_ac - can - to_al_ fuo - co - sta - rò___

lun - go_____ pal - pi - tar.   Ah fu un

lam - - po,   un so-gno, un giuo - -

co,   ah fu un lam-po, un so-gno, un giuo - co_ il_ mi - o_____

lun - - go_____ pal - - pi -

Il segreto per esser felici

from
LUCREZIA BORGIA

Gaetano Donizetti

Il se - gre-to per es-ser fe - li - ci so per

pro - va e l'in - se - gno a - gli a - mi — — ci. Sia se - re - no, sia nu - bi - lo il

cie — lo, o - gni tem - po, sia cal - do, sia ge - lo, scher - zo e

be - vo, e de - ri - do gl'in - sa - ni che si dan del fu - tu - ro pen -

sier. _____ Scher - zo e be - vo, e de - ri - do gl'in - sa - ni che __ si

da - to go - der,_____ n'è

Allegretto

da - to go - der.

Pro-fit - tia-mo degl' an - ni fio - ren - ti; il pia - cer li fa cor-rer più

len - ti. Se vec - chiez - za con li - vi - da fac - cia stam-mi a

ter - go e mia vi - ta mi - nac - cia, scher - zo e be - vo, e de - ri - do gl'in-

sa - ni che si dan del fu - tu - ro pen - sier. Scher - zo e

be - vo, e de - ri - do gl'in - sa - ni che si dan del fu - tu - ro pen -

sier. Non cu - ria - mo l'in - cer - to do -

Nobles seigneurs, salut!

from
LES HUGUENOTS

Giacomo Meyerbeer

hom - me qu'elle a ___ choi - si, qu'elle a ___ choi - si! ___

cresc. e stacc.   *dim. e legato*   *cresc. e stacc.*   *dim. e legato*

Vous pou - vez croi - re que nul ___ sei - gneur n'eut tant de gloi - re ni de ___ bon - heur,

cresc.   *cresc.*

p   *p*

n'eut ___ tant de gloi - re, tant de gloi - re, de bon -

p

heur,   non, non, non, non, non, non, non, non, non, non, ___ non, ___ ja -

O mio Fernando!

from
LA FAVORITA

Gaetano Donizetti

nor — no, ma - i; do - ves - se e - se - crar - mi, fug - gir, sa - prà in brev'

o - ra chi sia la don - na che co - tan - to a - do - ra.

a piacere

Andante cantabile

Oh mio Fer - nan - do! Del - la ter - ra il tro - no

a pos - se - der - ti a - vri - a do - na - to il cor;

ma pu - ro l'a - mor mi - o co - me il per - do - no,

dan - na-to, ahi las - sa! è a di - spe - ra - to or - ror.

Il ver fia no - to, e in tuo dis - pre - gio e -

stre - mo, la pe - na a - vrom - mi

che mag- gior___ si de', ah!_____ Se il giu-sto tuo dis-

104

Su, cru - de - li, e chi v'ar - re - sta? Scrit - to è in
cie - lo il mio do - lor! Scrit - to è in ciel_____ il mio do -
lor!_____ Su, ve - ni - te, ell'è u - na fe - sta; spar - sa
l'a - ra sia di fior._____ Già la tom - ba a me s'ap -

* a cut is usually made to the *Moderato mosso* four pages ahead, marked **

pre - sta; ri - co - per - ta in ne - gro vel___ sia la

tri - sta fi - dan - za - ta che re - iet - ta, di - spe -

ra - ta, non a - vrà___ per - do - no in ciel. Ma - le - det -

ta, di - spe - ra - ta, non a - vrà per - do - no in ciel, no,___ non a -

vrà, ma - le - det - - ta, di - spe - ra - - ta, non a - vrà per - do - no in

ciel, non a - vrà per - do - no in ciel, ah!_____ non a - vrà per - do - no in

Allegro

ciel.

Ah!_____ cru - de - li e chi_____ v'ar - re - sta?

Scrit - to in cie - lo è il mio do - lor.

Scrit - to in cie - lo è il mio do - lor.

Cru -

de - li, ve - ni - te.

Tempo I

Scrit-to è in

108

Più mosso

vrà per-do - no in ciel. Ah! la tri - sta fi - dan -

za - ta non a - vrà, non a -

vrà per-do - no in ciel, ah non a -

vrà per-do - no in ciel, ah non a -

Stride la vampa!

from
IL TROVATORE

Giuseppe Verdi

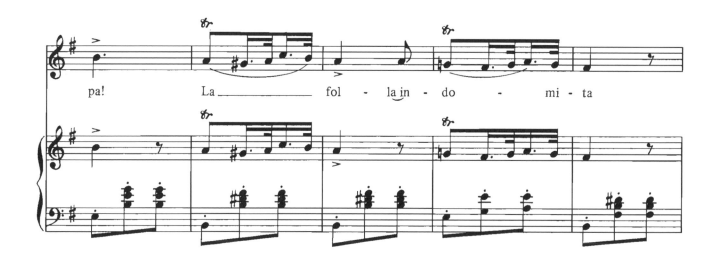

ta in sem - bian - za! Ur - li di

gio - ia in - tor - no ec - cheg - gia - no;

cin - ta di sgher - ri don -

na s'a - van - za! Si - ni - stra

di - scin - ta e scal - za! Gri -

do fe - ro - ce di _____ mor - te _____

marcato

pp

pp

le - va - si; l'e - co il ri - pe -

f

marcato

te di _____ bal - za in bal - za! Si -

Faites-lui mes aveux

from
FAUST

Charles Gounod

qu'il s'ex-hale a - vec vous_____ par - fums_____ plus doux!_____

dim.

p

Andante   Recit.

Fa -

cresc.

f

né - e!   Hé - las!   ce sor - cier,   que Dieu dam - ne,   m'a por - té mal -

colla voce

Tempo I

heur!_____

p

cresc.

fa - nent? Non! Sa - tan, je ris de

pp molto cresc.

Tempo I Allegretto

toi! C'est en vous que j'ai foi; par -

dim. *p*

stacc.

lez pour moi! Qu'el - le puis - se con -

naî - tre l'é - moi qu'elle a fait naî - tre,

cresc.

et dont mon cœur trou - blé_____ n'a point_____ par -

lé!_____ C'est en vous que j'ai foi;_____ par - lez_____ pour

pp

moi!_____ Si l'a - mour l'ef - fa - rou - che,

que la fleur sur sa bou - che sa - che au moins dé - po -

cresc.

Que fais-tu, blanche tourterelle

from

ROMÉO ET JULIETTE

Charles Gounod

Allegretto (♩ = 84)

Recit. Moderato
STEPHANO:

De - puis hi - er je cher-che en vain mon maî - tre! Est - il en - core chez

vous, Mes - sei - gneurs Ca - pu - let?_____ Voy-ons un peu si vos di - gnes va -

lets à ma voix ce ma - tin o - se - ront re - pa - raî - tre!

Allegretto (♩ = 88)

Poco meno mosso (♩ = 72)

Que fais - tu, blan - che tour - te - rel - le,

dans ce nid de vau - tours?_____ Quel - que jour, dé - ploy - ant ton

ré - e; leurs chan-sons que fuit Cy-thé-ré - e ré -

son - nent à grand bruit!_____ Ce-pen-dant, en leur douce_i-

vres-se nos a-mants con-tent leur_ten-dres-se aux

as-tres de la nuit!_____ Gar-dez bien la_

bel - le, Qui vi - vra ver - ra! Vo - tre____ tour - te -

rel - le vous é - chap - pe - ra, vo - tre____ tour - te -

rel - le____ vous____ é - chap - pe - ra! Gar-dez bien la bel -

Più lento

le! Vo-tre tour-te- rel - le vous é-chap - pe- ra!

Chacun à son goût

from
DIE FLEDERMAUS

Johann Strauss

134

je - mand hier bei mir, so pack' ich ihn ganz
zie - ret wie ein Tropf, dem wer - fe ich ganz
un - ge - niert— werf ihn hin - aus zur Tür, so
un - ge - niert die Fla - sche an den Kopf, dem
pack' ich ihn ganz un - ge - niert— werf ihn hin - aus zur
wer - fe ich ganz un - ge - niert die Fla - sche— an den
f
Tür.— Und fra - gen— Sie, ich bit - te, wa -
Kopf.— Und fra - gen— Sie, ich bit - te, wa -
pp

L'amour est un oiseau rebelle
(Habanera)

from
CARMEN

Georges Bizet

t'ai - me; mais si je t'ai - me, si je

t'ai - me, prends garde ___ a toi! ___

L'oi - seau que tu croy - ais sur -

pren - dre bat - tit de l'aile ___ et ___ s'en - vo - la. L'a - mour

Près des remparts de Séville
(Seguidilla)

from
CARMEN

Georges Bizet

Allegretto (♪ = 160)

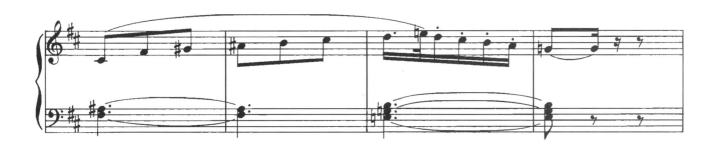

CARMEN:

Près des rem - parts de Sé - vil - le,

144

chez—mon a - mi— Lil - las Pas - tia,_____ j'i -

rai dan - ser la Sé - gue - dille et boi - re du man - za -

nil - la._____ J'i - rai chez mon a - mi Lil - las

Pas - tia._____

sempre pp

sempre pp

Oui,— mais tou - te seule on s'en - nui - e, et les vrais plai - sirs

sont à deux;—— donc,— pour me te - nir com - pa - gni - e, j'em -

mè - ne - rai mon a - mou - reux!——————— Mon a - mou -

p

ten.

au bon mo - ment!___ Je n'ai guè - re le temps d'at -

ten - dre, car a - vec mon nou-vel a - mant ___

f *e ben ritmato*

près des rem - parts de Sé - vil - le,

chez___ mon a - mi___ Lil - las Pas - tia,___

En vain, pour éviter

from
CARMEN

Georges Bizet

La mort! J'ai bien lu— moi d'a-bord, en - sui - te lui—

pour tous les deux, la mort!—

Andante molto moderato (♩ = 66)

En vain, pour é - vi - ter les ré - pon - ses a - mè - res, en vain tu

mê - le - ras! _____ Ce - la ne sert à rien; les car - tes sont sin -

cè - res et ne men - ti - ront pas! _____ Dans le li - vre d'en

haut si ta page est heu - reuse, mêle et cou - pe sans peur: _____

poco sf *pp*

la car - te sous tes doigts se tour - ne - ra joy - eu - se, t'an - non - çant

le bon - heur! _____ Mais si tu dois mou - rir— si le mot re - dou -

ta - ble est é - crit par le sort—— re - com - men - ce vingt

fois, la carte im - pi - to - ya - ble ré - pé - te - ra: la mort! _____

poco cresc.

cresc. molto

Oui, si tu dois mou - rir, re - com - men - ce vingt fois, _____

cresc.

ff

f

dim.

Voce di donna

from
LA GIOCONDA

Amilcare Ponchielli

te - ne - bre di quel - la__ san - ta, di quel - la san - ta il vol - to,

col canto   *morendo*

a tempo   *affrett.*

pu - re da me non par - ta - si, da me non

p a tempo   *affrett.*

par - ta - si, sen - za un pie - to - so don,   no!   no! _____ A

col canto

a tempo

te que - sto ro - sa - rio   che le pre-ghie-re a -

pp leggerissime

mi - a be - ne - di - zion.

La mia be - ne - di - zion vi - gi - li,_____ vi - gi -

li, ah! sul - la tua te - sta vi - gi - li la mi - a

be - ne - di - zion._____

Printemps qui commence

from

SAMSON ET DALILA

Camille Saint-Saëns

Prin - temps qui com - men - ce, por-

tant l'es-pé - ran - ce aux cœurs a - mou-reux, ton

souf - fle qui pas - se de la terre ef - fa - ce les jours mal-heu - reux.

Tout brûle en notre â - me, et ta dou-ce

flam - me vient sé - cher nos pleurs; tu

rends à la ter - re, par un doux mys-tè - - re,

cresc. **Poco animato**

les fruits et les fleurs. En vain je suis bel - le! Mon

cœur plein d'a-mour, pleu - rant l'in - fi - dèle, at - tend son re-

tour! Vi - vant d'es - pé - ran - ce, mon cœur dé - so-

lé   gar - de sou - ve - nan - ce   du bon-heur pas-

sé!

Andante (♩ = 84)

A

la nuit tom-ban - te j'i - rai, triste a - man - te,

m'as-seoir au tor - rent, l'at-tendre en pleu - rant! Chas -

sant ma tris - tes - se, s'il re-vient un jour, à lui ma ten -

dres - se et la douce i - vres - se qu'un brû -

Amour! viens aider ma faiblesse!

from
SAMSON ET DALILA

Camille Saint-Saëns

doit sa - tis - fai - re nos dieux!

mour! viens ai - der ma fai - bles - se!

Ver - se le poi - son dans son sein!

Fais que, vain - cu par mon a - dres - se, Sam -

son soit en - chaî - né_____ de - main!

Il vou - drait en vain___ de son â - me pou-

accel.
cresc.
roux; moi seule, en-tre tous, je le
accel.
pp
cresc.
[ten.]
Opt.
6
f
3
bra - - - ve, et le re-
f
p
tiens à mes ge - noux!
cresc.
[a tempo]
3
3
f
A - mour! viens ai - der ma fai - bles -
f
p

se!   Ver - se le poi - son dans   son sein!

Fais   que,   vain - cu   par mon a -

dres   -   se,   Sam - son soit en - chaî -

né ____ de - main!   Con - tre l'a -

mour, sa force est vai - ne; et

lui, le— fort par - mi les forts — lui, qui d'un

peu - ple rompt la chaî - ne, suc - com - be -

ra — sous mes — ef - forts!

Mon cœur s'ouvre à ta voix

from
SAMSON ET DALILA

Camille Saint-Saëns

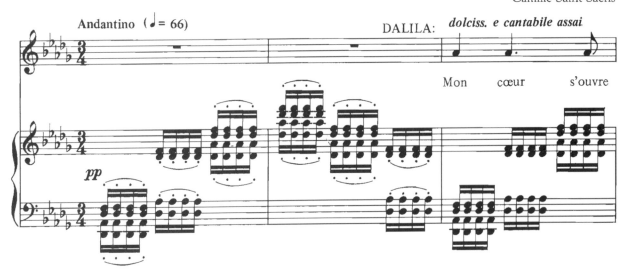

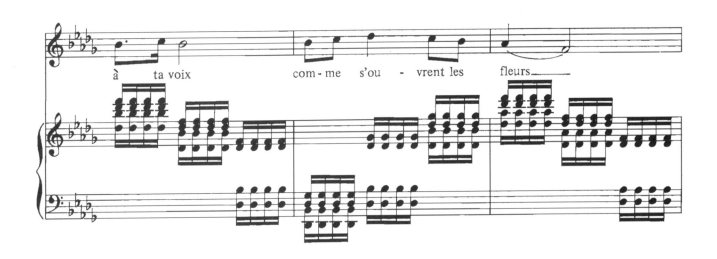

Mais, ô mon bien - ai - mé,

pour mieux sé - cher mes pleurs,____ que ta voix____

parle en - co - re! Dis -

moi qu'à Da - li - la tu re - viens pour ja -

ain - si   fré - mit mon cœur,

prêt à se con - so - ler _____

à ta voix _____   qui m'est chè - re!

Voi lo sapete

from
CAVALLERIA RUSTICANA

Pietro Mascagni

ter - na fè giu - ra - to, a - ve - va a Lo - la e -

ter - na fè giu - ra - to._____ Tor - nò, la sep - pe

spo - sa; e con un nuo - vo a - mo - re_____

_ vol - le spe - gner la fiam - ma che gli bru - cia - va il

Va! laisse couler mes larmes

from
WERTHER

Jules Massenet

188

Acerba voluttà

from
ADRIANA LECOUVREUR

Francesco Cilea

Largo (♩ = 126)

pp e cupo

Agitato (♩ = 84)

O - gni e - co, o - gni om - bra nel - la

not - te in - ce - sa con - tro la im-pa-

zien - te al - ma con - giu - ra:

fra dub - biez - za   e   de - sì - o   tut - ta so -

spe - sa,   l'e - ter - ni - tà___ nell' at - ti - mo   mi - su - ra.

Con moto (♩ = 176)

pp leggerissimo

ver - so, mi - sto al so - spir d'un ar - bo - re dor - men - te.

Sostenuto (♩ = 69)

O va - ga - bon - da stel - la d'O - ri -

en - te, non tra - mon - tar,

non tra - mon - tar; sor - ri -

We cannot retrace our steps

from
THE MOTHER OF US ALL

Virgil Thomson

200

Lullaby

from
THE CONSUL

Gian Carlo Menotti

lamb and dove. I shall buy for you sug-ar and bread.

Sleep, my love, sleep for me. My sleep is

dead._____ Rain will fall but

mf movendo un poco

Ba — by won't know, He laughs a - lone in or - chards of gold.

Ah, Michele, don't you know

from

THE SAINT OF BLEECKER STREET

Gian Carlo Menotti

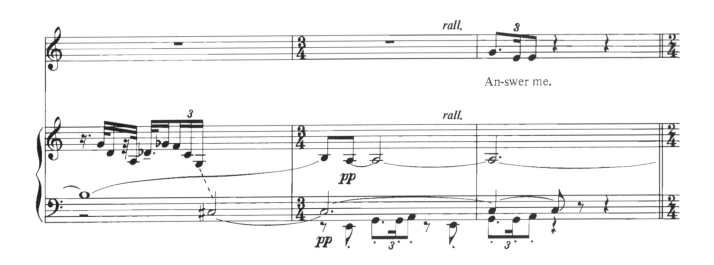

tears are mir - rored, can bear the se - cret pain of liv - ing.

Those of us,___ who find our love on earth,___ must cel - e - brate___ our fleet - ing

tri - umph. Who wel - comes love in si - lence or hides it like a

crime, shall soon run to the waste - lands to es - cape its blind - ing

Augusta! How can you turn away?

from
THE BALLAD OF BABY DOE

Douglas Moore

Can this be you, Au - gus - ta? Do you not know

Hor-ace Ta - bor? Is he less _____ than a stran-ger?

Allegro appassionato

Go to him now, Au - gus - ta. Hold out your hand to

him. _____ For - get your pride; he is in trou - ble.

214

The years of bit-ter-ness, Years of emp-ti-ness and

heart - break, All these must pass _____ for-got-ten

now, Now that he needs you, Au - gus - ta.

Ta - bor, my hus-band! Ta - bor, my dear one! Why, why did you ev - er

Must the winter come so soon?

from
VANESSA

Samuel Barber

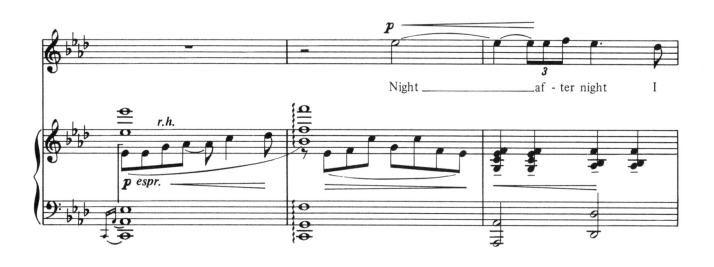

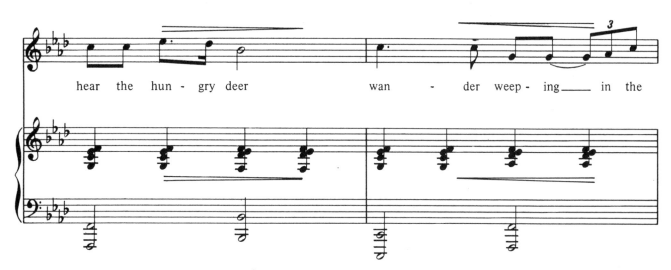

woods,_____ and__ from his house of brit-tle bark__

hoots__ the fro - zen owl. Must the win-ter__ come so

soon? Here _____

_____ in this for - est nei-ther dawn__ nor sun - set

marks the pas-sing____ of the days.____

It is a long win-ter here.

Must the win-ter____ come so soon?____